Conversations with Athena at Mieza

poems by

Silvia Scheibli

Finishing Line Press
Georgetown, Kentucky

Conversations with Athena at Mieza

Copyright © 2022 by Silvia Scheibli
ISBN 978-1-64662-945-9 First Edition
All rights reserved under International and Pan-American Copyright Conventions. No part of this book may be reproduced in any manner whatsoever without written permission from the publisher, except in the case of brief quotations embodied in critical articles and reviews.

ACKNOWLEDGMENTS

The poems in this book appeared in the following publications. Grateful acknowledgement is made to the editors of these publications:

Ann Arbor Review: "In Buddha's Garden," "The Sacred Pool," "Before Breakfast," "After Breakfast" and "The Banquet"
The Bitter Oleander: "Athena," "Leaves in the Shape of Water," "Returning to Hera's Garden," and "Baking Bread"
Cholla Needles: "Seventeen Raindrops," "Where were you, asks Athena," "Athena's Mother, Hera," "Athena's Sketch on Corfu 1," "Athena's Sketch on Corfu 2," "Athena's Sketch on Corfu 3" and "Athena's Sketch on Corfu 4"
January Review: "Macedonia," "Mieza, Sanctuary of Nymphs," "Sappho," "Oracle at Delphi" and "Hermes"
Osiris: "Odysseus' Dilemma"

Publisher: Leah Huete de Maines
Editor: Christen Kincaid
Cover Art: José Rodeiro, *PRANCE*, http://www.rodeiro-art.com/
Author Photo: Roy G. Rodriguez
Cover Design: Elizabeth Maines McCleavy

Order online: www.finishinglinepress.com
also available on amazon.com

Author inquiries and mail orders:
Finishing Line Press
PO Box 1626
Georgetown, Kentucky 40324
USA

Table of Contents

Introduction by Patty Dickson Pieczka 1
Athena 3
Leaves in the Shape of Water 4
Seventeen Raindrops 5
Where were you, asks Athena 6
Athena's Mother, Hera 7
Athena's Sketch on Corfu #1 8
Athena's Sketch on Corfu #2 9
Athena's Sketch on Corfu #3 10
Athena's Sketch on Corfu #4 11
In Buddha's Garden 12
The Sacred Pool 13
Before Breakfast 14
After Breakfast 15
The Banquet 16
Macedonia 17
Mieza, Sancuary of Nymphs 18
Sappho 19
Oracle at Delphi 20
Hermes 21
The Code 22
Returning to Hera's Garden 23
Hermes' Song in the Underworld 24
Athena's Ode to Aphrodite 25
Aphrodite, Psyche and Eros 26
Baking Bread 27
Odysseus' Love Song 28
Odysseus' Dilemma 29
Epilogue 30

INTRODUCTION

After dipping a toe into the clear pool of Silvia Scheibli's latest collection, *Conversations with Athena*, it is impossible to resist the desire to immerse oneself completely in its healing waters. Silvia's writing appears effortless. She and Athena become one as:

> Athena asked herself
> why lyrics
> seemed to write themselves
> like transparent silhouettes
> of minnows.

Nature vines itself throughout this book as it pertains to inspiration and spiritual awareness. These exquisite and sensitive poems explore sensuality in a journey of self-realization. Athena's tribulations are easily translatable into the modern world, as Silvia and Athena confront relationships between mother and daughter, a strong woman's place in a hyper-masculine society, Athena's relationship with the poet Sappho, and Athena's methods of dealing with her father, Zeus, while avoiding his wrath.

Before meeting Hera, we're introduced to Gaia, the mother of all life:

> The first mother calls Athena
> with white daisies
> buttery yellow centers
> cobalt blue gentians
> and forget-me-not blues.
>
> By roadside grasses Gaia tells her
> she is an artist
> how rainwater and mud
> inspire her to paint pink snails.

Silvia's words evoked magic in several poems, such as, "Where Were You, asks Athena:"

> Where were you?
> When a round stone
> became a hedgehog and
> buried my poem in her den

And again in, "The Code:"

> Purring &
> Without angering Zeus
> Athena transforms herself
> Into one of Sappho's cats
> She keeps by her side
>
> A golden-eyed calico
> Whose face with black
> Heart-shaped mask
> Tantalizes dancers

To read Silvia Scheibli's work is to experience the sensation of watching these ancient and imaginative events play out in person, so visual and creative is her writing. Each word is as light as breath, and:

> each breath is like
> a blue horse
> prancing into the future.

—**Patty Dickson Pieczka**
Author of *Beyond the Moon's White Claw*

Athena

The first mother calls Athena
with white daisies
buttery yellow centers
cobalt blue gentians
and forget-me-not blues

By road-side grasses Gaia tells her
she is an artist
how rain water and mud
inspire her to paint pink snails

She says she likes being a poet
and sends words on the wind
to friends in both worlds
so that they could remember her
even though some could not see
far beyond clouds, forests or rivers
but sometimes reached her spirit
in her sleep

She says
it is easy to forget
how thunder and lightening
sharpened her spirit

Even the coyote
recognizes her, she said,
leaves her alone
when morning clouds come
to help her work with her hands
and send messages

Leaves in the shape of water

Athena stretched
tracing the stream's voice with her fingers
leaves in the shape of water
on crystal sand

Her ankles sank
into the quixotic river bank
where phoebes wrote poems

Athena asked herself
why lyrics
seemed to write themselves
like transparent silhouettes
of minnows

She wished her verdant blood
would mingle with silken shadows
of jade cottonwoods

Seventeen Raindrops

It wasn't the seventeen raindrops
or the feint rumblings of thunder

No

It was more like weeds steadily thriving
while catnip, oregano and parsley dried up
that suddenly reminded
Athena of her heart
giving in to extreme and unrelenting heat
blinding her ever stealthy
movements

Her motion
memories and now
these moments
all interwoven somehow
pushing vivid dreams
on an astral plane
forming an anonymous smile
parting lips ever so slightly

Her breath
coming more and more
deeply
with the blurry touch of
rain

Where were you, asks Athena

When snow flowers
emerged through ice and diamonds
grew around each green stem

When hazel nuts
shed fuzzy caps and blackberries
scraped sugar from my lips

Where were you?

When a round stone
became a hedgehog and
buried my poem in her den

When tomato plants
leaned against the woodshed
for balance

When a young apple tree's
bright branches
flirted with sunshine

Athena's Mother, Hera

I was very young, Athena,
my hair was glossy
my skin as tender as coriander
I searched in sand and
rain for my destiny

For words
as natural as breathing
as tantalizing
as sap flowing through willows

As insects wedged in amber
I tracked you in mud
thinking I had found you
but I was wrong

It was your birth, Athena,
that awakened me

Your birth was my birth
shaping my disposition
my enchantment
my infinite face

That you now see for yourself
facing these cliffs and sea
embellished in poppies
caressing April hillsides

Athena's Sketch on Corfu #1

Azul words
tumble in pale foam

Turtles read
green sunlight on algae

Sea birds dress
in orange-black perfume

A seedeater's
white collar
unfolds
on emerald bamboo

Not a single sad echo
reverberates from the past

Each breath is like
a blue horse
prancing into the future

Athena's Sketch on Corfu #2

An orange harvest moon
conspired
with thunder clouds
enticing dry ground
with a hard rain &
lightning

Crickets
missed by the chickens
& skinny-wild dogs
hunkered on wet sand
feeling tense

Athena's Sketch on Corfu #3

A milk-white morph butterfly
with silken wings
threw me a kiss
& a short warning
of sea monsters
submerged
in the mud of our dreams
waiting to drown all
in the endless
River Styx

Athena's Sketch on Corfu #4

"Kabir...Kabir"

Kingbirds'
raucous calls

"Kabir...Kabir"

Terrestrial cries
stirring clouds with burgundy
& golden hues

Transform
one-dimensional
right-brained mortals
into gods

Like
elemental words
aspiring mythical worlds
on this Greek Island

In Buddha's Garden

Athena walked with her father, Zeus,
not listening
to Olympian sagas he touted,
but admiring how the copper patina on statues
matched her mandarin ducks' feathers

She masked her expressions carefully
not wanting to annoy him
so she could pursue
her own musings

The irony did not escape her—
he himself had carefully taught
her how to hide her feelings
in plain sight—
insisting on being aware
of the other-
the ego or the alter-ego
depending on the
moment's agenda

She refrained from
indulging him with her weakness—the lovely scent of two
gardenias her lover had placed near her—or her father would
have found a way to
belittle her out of jealousy

The Sacred Pool

Athena swam in her sacred pool
hoping to envision once more
the lover
she had dreamt of decades ago
only to be distracted by
athletic feats
of the likes of Poseidon whom
her father adored
and wanted her to worship too

The scent of orange
and jasmine blossoms had saved her then
and now

Had given her the insight into one of her most
treasured tasks which was
to face her immortality
like a mortal would—
gently and kindly
but with one exception—
her heart
must remain whole

Before Breakfast

Athena
liked to see
herself
through her lovers'
eyes

Often
admired for the
deep cleft
of her breasts

Emphasized
by a crimson
caftan
she wore
carelessly

Tossing
her silken
hair
over
their
chests

After Breakfast

Athena brought
left-over pastries,
mangos
to her glossy Phoenix
anxious
knowing the damage
he could cause

Last summer
he torched
immense forests and she
had promised her brother
to contain him over-night
behind a waterfall
or he would transform him
into a jungle fowl

Secretly she loved
the ardent flames, ashes &
consumed promises
of an avant-guard
dawn

The Banquet

Remembering
tonight's banquet
honoring the hemlock crowd—
gray-beards
with pedophile tendencies—

Athena selected
a dazzling gown stitched by the
Pleiades' Seven Sisters
and given her by
Cronus and Rhea, her
grandparents

Being of the warrior caste
and a woman
she was excluded from
attending Hemlock Society meetings

Only because of her
mother Hera's reputation,
gray-beards lined up for
oysters and langostino hors d'oeuvres
as well as glimpses
of her brother, Apollo,
buffed in Orion's Belt

Macedonia

Although
Athena abhorred shopping
especially now
as the plague
raged in this spectral city
with centuries-old limestone benches
painted facades &
Hellenistic warriors mounted on
marble colonnades

She hoped to discover
the latest palace intrigues
of strategic marriages & diplomacy
so characteristic of this
hyper-masculine society

Also she needed to find
a lion skin headdress
to bribe her brother
who believed that war brought glory
so that she could pursue
her secret pan-ethic studies
at her sanctuary
in Vergina

Mieza Sanctuary of Nymphs

Athena felt safe at Mieza

Evading her father's security detail
eluding one or two still glowing funeral pyres
after the latest blood-sport intrigue at the palace
she was elated to arrive
at the caves and hidden springs
of Mieza

Here Athena sought out
Sappho, who with her own circle
of poets and artists,
knew more ethics and philosophy
than anyone she had ever met—
being in her presence was itself
a symposium

Sappho

Much beloved
admired and slandered
Sappho had promised to meet her
in the peristyle whose mosaic floor
was created entirely of polished beach pebbles
in a botanical motif
with jade, emerald and cerulean hues
accenting the deeper greens
of the Mieza's lush, wind-combed grasses

Her star-warmed eyes
met Athena's at breaking point
beyond which nothing felt real
except the inlaid fire of
imagination &
insight

Oracle at Delphi

Quivering
Sappho and Athena
travelled to Athens
crossing pomegranate-studded terrain
to Delphi
where the oracle's hand-raised goats
roamed ancient olive groves

Intending to learn their fortunes
they assisted with
washing bones in rubescent wine
wrapping them in purple cloth &
placing them in a golden larnax
inside a marble sarcophagus
before sealing the tomb

While the god Hermes
conducted the warrior's soul
to the underworld

Hermes

Deciding to join the party
Hermes stirred Sappho's pulse
undressing her mind
with quips, quotes & gossip

Leaving Athena to socially
distance and daydream about
twirling those ebony loose curls
at Sappho's serene temple

They toasted their friendship
with Campari
enjoying bowls of saffron rice
with squid, mussels and clams

For dessert
Sappho read poems about her
newest lover
who slept all day &
would only pee in a silver vessel
handed to her by a young page
wearing scarlet slippers
embossed with golden
Phainopeplas

The Code

Aching
to avow her love
the Olympian Code inhibits
Athena from voicing
bougainvilleas blazing
in her skin

Her sullen lips implore
the fog-patched Capri sky
not to betray her

Purring &
without angering Zeus
Athena transforms herself
into one of Sappho's cats
she keeps by her side

A golden-eyed calico
whose face with black
heart-shaped mask
tantalizes dancers

Playing a seven-string lyre
Sappho's artful fingers
melt Athena's blood
like moonlit glitter
on a stormless sea

Returning to Hera's Garden

I need to hear the mother's voice

The gentle sweet caress
of her pale hands
soothing my shoulders

The light curls reflecting the love
only she expressed

I miss her
never clear in daylight
yet dazzling under the cherry tree
shaking with the moon's gaze

Yes,
I must return
to the garden's fragrance
asleep on rose petals

Nothing need be hidden

All echos young and old
revealed

Pain will rise up and fly off

Like a dove
bursting from the shade

Hermes' Song in the Underworld

Death's gifts
are not so many

Yet stillness is supreme

No blossom quite so poignant

No leaf so green
as greener providence

Death's gifts
are not so many

Yet silence is supreme

No blossom quite so fragrant

No tree so green
as greener deity

Athena's Ode to Aphrodite

It just isn't in you, Aphrodite,
hiding flaming eyes
& fragrant sensibilities
in a torrid deluge of wanting

Your primal gaze rivals
the Autumnal tide that
can not diverge or deviate
from mirroring your yearning

You cannot stand still
revealing feverish hills &
graceful gardens breathing
Star Jasmine-scented desire

Aphrodite
no one is spared—
demi-god, mortal, immortal
or goddess—
from brimming over
with immanent longing
to glimpse your dark soul
in Eros' elated arms

Aphrodite, Psyche & Eros

Like two quivering butterflies
on a golden hibiscus
Aphrodite & Eros
draw a line in the sand
while Psyche sleeps

Their eight daughters
seek refuge
seek Athena's shield
against hate, injustice &
pimping Cupid

Lost on Cypress Cliffs
above tide pools
Psyche is speechless
seeing Aphrodite
digging for clams
wearing only foam and
seaweed clinging to thighs
alluring, wild, blonde curls
in Eros' embrace

Athena & distraught daughters
watch chariot races in Lindos

Baking Bread

Occasionally on hot summer nights
Athena liked to bake bread

She felt the knot of anxiety fade
and serenity's mild, inward flow
cling like flour to ringless fingers

She recognized the delicate
rising and falling of her chest
by the definitive kneading
of her thoughts

She knew
she touched stillness
the instant yeast mixed with water

The round glass bowl fit her vision
of a harmonious society perfectly

Pain, suffering and hunger
were deflected by its earthly shape

An intense realization of her grounding will
determined her next move on Mount Olympus

Odysseus' Love Song

Athena,
my yearning
    leans lightly
on eyelids

Your glance
    fills my veins
with half-
       closed lashes
like a willet's lost cry
    by sea foam

Castanets…the breeze

….guitars

whisper my sighs' secrets

       overwhelm
               memories
……overwhelm

Odysseus' Dilemma

Your loyalty

      is an invisible cloak

over my shoulders,

Athena

      and although

I can only envision you

    help me intuit

which part of your body

      is your favorite

so I can dream

    in peace

touch the sandy shore of your hips

      like a wayward seabird

with salty memories

      on my tongue

EPILOGUE

At the River bank

Athena slipped on wet sand
ferns and moss
flooded her veins

Water brushed her hair
she felt feathers ruffle
her face and arms

As she focused on her reflection
in the stream's ripples,
a black swan bathed

Sunlight fell
from tall cottonwoods
scattering calls of water birds

Shadows emerged
strengthening her
primordial being

Silvia Scheibli has served as judge for the 2017 Bitter Oleander Press Library of Poetry Book Award. In 2015 she was invited to Ecuador in a cultural exchange of poets between the United States and Ecuador touring and reciting in the Amazonas as well as Quito, Babajoyo and Guayaquil with Alan Britt and Steve Barfield. Besides publishing eight books of poems including, *The Moon Rises in the Rattlesnake's Mouth*, by Bitter Oleander Press, *Under the Loquat Tree* in 2002 by Vida Publishing and *Parabola Dreams* co-authored with Alan Britt in 2013 by Bitter Oleander Press, she is the editor and publisher of Cypress Review and Cypress Books since 1980.

Graduate of the University of Tampa, Tampa, Florida, in the late 60's she studied with Duane Locke, founder of the Immanentist Movement in poetry. Along with Paul Roth, Alan Britt, Steve Barfield, José Rodeiro and others, the Immanentist movement still thrives today in the United States, Europe and South America and everywhere where a visionary approach focuses on primordial nature similar to the surrealism and Deep Image poetry of Federico Garcia Lorca, Pablo Neruda, Karl Krolow and others. Immanentist poems and paintings are embedded with passion and inspiration and loved for their universal Duende qualities.

She has published poems in *Cholla Needles, Osiris, Bitter Oleander, Ann Arbor Review, Black Moon, The Midwest Quarterly, The January Review* and *The Raw Seed Review* among others. She is an enthusiastic photographer and birder living near the borderlands in southeast Arizona where jaguars, bobcats, coatimundi, white-tailed deer and javelina move freely.

www.ingramcontent.com/pod-product-compliance
Lightning Source LLC
LaVergne TN
LVHW041511070426
835507LV00012B/1487